Gabriel's Wing

Poems by Allan Cooper

GASPEREAU PRESS PRINTERS & PUBLISHERS MMIV

"Grief is the price you pay for love."

—RABBI EARL GROLLMAN

He lay resting in the snow. His weary limbs had grown light and his inflamed eyes smiled.

When he closed them to sleep a little, he still heard God's voice speaking and still looked into His bright eyes.

"So you've nothing more to complain about?" God's voice asked.

"Nothing more," Knulp nodded with a shy laugh.

"And everything's all right? Everything is as it should be?"

"Yes," he nodded. "Everything is as it should be."

God's voice became softer. Now it sounded like his mother's voice, now like Henriette's, and now like the good gentle voice of Lisabeth.

—FROM *KNULP*, BY HERMANN HESSE

THIS BOOK IS
FOR LAURIE & KATIE
& ROBERT HAWKES
WITH LOVE

The Driftwood Man

The potatoes grow
in neat rows
beside the brook.
The earth
breathes evenly.
That was years ago.
Worries and cares
lived in comic books
and old novels,
and we
lived them too.
                    Inside
the cabin, silence,
the driftwood man
rowing
toward who knows
what shore.
Listen
to the slow waves
of sorrow
rising from his chest.
We all feel it
in the aloneness,
so beautiful,
breaking the soul
nearly
in two.

My friend,
it's time
to drink
from the same cup.
The last notes
of the flute
are sombre
and low. Then
we'll sleep alone
all night beside the ocean.

Opening a Door

I walk across the porch and open the door.
Night sounds come in, the scent
of rose petals mixed with rain.
Someone is walking toward me,
but there's no sound of footsteps,
no steps at all. The street dark,
the night cool, clouds above the moon
like a young woman's face.
I went over and opened the door
so that everything cool and lovely
and lost could come home again.

I don't think I meant to come here,
it just happened. Was it passion,
or some messenger from the other world,
longing to be reborn?
We're all agents of the unexpected,
especially between dusk and dawn.
That's when they appear in the room
and walk through the wall,
almost as if it doesn't exist.
They're determined to be somewhere else,
but they give us a glimpse.
It's a feeling we wake with
in the morning:
"Someone's expecting us.
It's time to go."

My friend, we make what we want
of the world—the oak tree,
and the shadows of the oak tree
moving in wind. We make
the wind fall, and the shadows still.
We walk home
in the melancholy of dusk,
the old aloneness. We decide
what to choose: apple or orange,
the face of the woman
blazing into light. But what we
choose decides to accept us
or not. We lie down,
fold our hands so.
The crickets sing all night.
The heaviness of the world
slips away for a little while.
Nothing less, and nothing more.

THE PLATE

Sometimes too many things
are piled on our plate—you know,
family, jobs, the old depression.
This goes on for days.
Nothing helps. We sing
and a glass falls from the cupboard.
We dance, and the dance floor
gives way. It's okay. Something
in the creak of the door as we open it
says we're not needed here;
we should be somewhere else.
So we walk, balancing the plate.
But we have to be careful:
if one thing falls, the world
as we know it goes with it.

I need more closeness
as I get older.
I follow the cats,
my wife and daughter
like the melancholy friend
in the old novel I love.
It's got something to do
with age, as if part of me
were slowly slipping
into the other world.

*

There are faces in senior's homes
folded with light. One smile
and they smile back at you,
dissolving the ballast
of anger and grief,
bearing lanterns
from this world
to the next.

*

Each glance we give
is a board
in the shed of love.
They're going up all the time,
everywhere in the world.
It's not lost yet.
Good things happen
and you feel them, here
in your chest.

THE THIN PLACES

In the thin places
I sit again with my father
and the words he gave me—
love, grace, patience, hope—
open like light through heavy curtains.

In the thin places
the love between two people
moves like amoebae
on slides of glass, changes,
meshes, like hands enfolding hands.

In the thin places
the yellow cat—sick
for two years—is whole again,
comes back to the house, says
"This is what I lived for."

In the thin places
time is a healing time,
and what is torn is mended,
and what has been given to you
is handed back to the world.

TWO LOVE POEMS

1.

This is the small farm of love.
The soil breathes and breathes all night.
In the first light, as the heron rises
wings open, close, open, in the other world.

2.

Love is the unformed haze
rising through the poppies
and the eyes, weeping, see it.

SMALL BOY AND LEAVES

A small boy is talking to the leaves.
What he's doing makes utter sense
in a world where no one
talks to anyone anymore.
A little breeze rises, and the boy says
"Come on, you can do it."
A cat jumps out of the leaves
onto the boy's shoulder.
He'll carry her home as she
nurses a sore paw, licking
and licking, eyes half-closed.
What they feel for each other
brings the two worlds close,
mends grief and loss and pain.
Together they're stitching the love
the world needs in order to survive.

HOPE

The body knows when desire,
that excited guest, arrives.
And fear shakes the rafters,
like thunder, like love.
When the dust settles
we ask where we are,
and our wits fly
back into our body.

A little voice starts up
from the corner,
from the cobwebs and dust.
Then there's a long
pause, a silence.
For hope
is the last thing we have,
and we cling to it.

Lovers join hands in the dark.
It's as simple as sunrise, complicated
as a sudden summer storm.
Big raindrops fall.
A face raised to the sky
can be filled
to the brim with joy.
The crickets feel it,
and the grass,
and the yellow blossoms
of the birdsfoot trefoil,
saying yes to the earth.

POTATOES

—for Seamus Heaney

Eyes growing beneath the earth,
moist, round stones
that have been here
as long
as the earth remembers—
break a new potato
open in your hands
and the bland rivers
run again, down your palm,
your fingers, back to the waiting earth.

*

My grandfather grew potatoes
in neat rows beside the brook
until a freshet took the field away.
His pipe smoke
lifted through the alders, the smell
of newly turned soil, and the sweat
on his brow moistened his cap
as he bent over the rows,
placing the seedlings deep in their beds.

*

There are fields we nourish inside us,
rows of light, double rows of grief.
And songs as old as the earth herself,
wholly given by the soil.
And what of the one word
we've longed for all our days?
What will we do when we find it?
A thin strand
leading all the way back to the Incas
rises in our planting.

The best days don't begin
with grand pronouncements.
It's when the cats are content
and the house glows
like the inside of a honeycomb.
Jake sleeps stretched out on the floor
while the big male, Mira, watches her
and preens. He has been something
wholly given to me, like true love,
or a gift you didn't expect or deserve.
The best days begin
when something inside begins to glow
like the light from a single cell.

Just when you think
the day's complete, the phone rings
with some disaster, or you step
into a bowl of milk. It's all right.
That sock you've been missing
is already home. It's the last
piece of the puzzle.
All you have to do is find it
and put it in its place.

GREEN EARS OF WHEAT

—after the painting by Vincent Van Gogh

There are openings to the other world through the green ears
of wheat. Haven't we always suspected this?

Especially when the rain falls in slanted bars
across the open sky, the opened heart.

For hearts, like wheat
are meant for bending.

How much can we take?
"Bring on the wind," whispers the wheat.

The Heaven of Loss

FACES

I see faces all the time
that move me. It's in the way
the light touches a cheek
or sets fire to the eyes
or deepens
a forehead furrowed
with grief.
          Very
few of these people
are beautiful in the way
the glossies
demand. You see them
walking out of theatres
or corner stores,
distant cousins
you've longed for all your life.
Some seem stricken
as if they can't understand
how they got here,
can't understand why
the cats left,
the lover.
Sometimes
one is weeping,
and you don't
turn away.

You touch
them on the shoulder,
tell them it's all right,
we'll get through this
together.

A woman is trying
hard to remember
something, trying
to find her way
back down the maze
of language
to a word
gone as sure
as a photograph
of an old friend
from school.
               What
does the word love
mean? Don't caring
and tenderness
accrue to it
like bits of earthly
dust? "Help me,"
she says. We pick
up the dictionary
and begin with
the letters of
the alphabet.
               "Does
it begin with a…e…t…?"
By the end
we're afraid
we might never
get it right.

It turns out to be
the name of
a friend,
and she remembers
it first: a sudden
victory.
　　　But what
does it mean
when language
abandons you
as completely
as a bitter friend?

There's so little love in the world
we have to make it ourselves,
shake off depression
like an old dog shaking off snow,
come inside and build a wood fire
in the heart.
                    When
I say "I love you"
I don't mean it lightly.
Years of caring go into it,
and grief and loss too.
                              I say
it now to everyone
in the same boat,
everyone
lost
or grieving
or alone—
love
going out
from this heart
broken over and over again.

Some day soon
I won't be here anymore.
I say 'soon',
but the days pile up
one after another
like leaves
or clouds
or snow.
    Where
did the time go?
At least we have memory,
that familiar friend,
and sometimes,
when he sees clearly,
the old days
shine again.
    It's
time to pack the car.
"See you, friend.
See you soon:"
we say this,
hoping
that it's true.

1.

I must've been six.
It was the toy department
at Eaton's,
and it was Christmas.
A small boy,
smaller than me,
was eating
an ice cream cone.
He was poor,
I could tell
by the smear of dirt
on his face
and his unkempt
hair. His mother
had him by the hand.
They turned a corner
quickly and the ice cream
sailed off the cone
to the floor.
I'd never seen a heart
broken like that before.
I'd never
seen a face
so sad.
I had one
chew of gum left,
and I reached deep

into my pocket
and gave it to him.
　　　　　Slowly
he stopped crying.
I never
saw him again.

2.

Whatever happened
to the cards
we traded
in grade school?
Whatever
happened to
Susan, the small
black-haired girl
I fell in love with
when I was ten?
Whatever happened
to Novella, the
the older girl
who babysat me?
I threw
book after book
down the stairs
with notes
floating out of them:
Novella, I love you.

Novella, come upstairs.
When her parents
moved away
my twelve-year-old
heart
broke in two, half
for mortal grief
and half for the heaven
of loss.

3.

Novella,
Susan,
where
did you go?
Where do we
all go
in the end,
when appointments
may not matter
anymore.
       But love
must be part of the
equation somehow,
some way. I can't think
of anything more
important to take
on the long

journey out of the self
than love,
mortal love,
the sounds of hearts
breaking
then opening again
in the other world.

The last page
isn't the end of the story.
There's always Knulp
in the snow,
talking to God,
making some peace
at last.
            Last words
fall light as snow,
accumulate,
take on layers
we don't understand
until years later.
Some of my
father's last
words to my mother
were "Muriel
I love you."
I think he also meant
he loved the feminine in her,
what was warm and caring,
and firm and determined
as well.
            He was certainly
resolved to go
somewhere
that morning
of his final waking.

                    The boat
should always
go out in peace,
the man or woman
at the helm,
those who left first
years ago
waiting
on the far shore
of the light.

Gabriel's Wing

The rain falls,
and falls
as it should,
in sudden big drops
that shake the rafters
or slow as can be,
misting
the fields,
each drop
waking
the music
of the leaves.
          When
I find I'm tired
out with too much
living, the rain
comes down.
When I find
I'm falling,
as we all fall
now and again—
nothing
seems right—
I reach out
for a face
or a hand
or the smallest
blue moth

and I'm steadied
again, feel
my feet firm
on the earth:
my friend,
we walk on, walk
on.

A POEM ABOUT BEARS

—for Robert Bly

Friend, we weren't the first
to weave this crazy quilt.
There's always Yeats and Stevens,
and our good friends Alden and James.

They would have badgered each other
until poems, filled with strange light,
suddenly appeared—having it out
with grief and sorrow, love and loss.

Alden was a bear. The bears around here
fatten on blueberries and sleep the whole winter.
Friend, while they're sleeping
we catch their breath in our words.

Having it out with sorrow and love:
more than this, our poems can become rafts
to carry our friends safely
to the other shore.

CLOTHESPINS

Everything counts.
It doesn't matter
if you're washing the clothes
or caught up in some corner
of the ecstatic;
it all adds up
to something.
                    It's like
a woman dancing:
at first
you see beauty,
then the movement,
then the form
behind the form.
                    Something
catches your eye—
a sheet flapping
in the wind,
held by one
corner.
Suddenly
you realize
it's your own soul.
When the last pin
snaps
you'll be free.

HONEYBEES

"The days you give me I give back to you."
—RUMI

1.

Whenever someone speaks
there's silence behind it, and the unseen.

But what about ecstatic love?
Nobody enters that door,

for it's already blown
off the hinges. Thresholds

don't matter anymore,
or taking off your shoes.

There's no time for proprieties.
One minute you're in this world

and then you're in the next.
Lovers stand cheek to cheek.

Nobody knows what they say.
But the sky

hears it, and the clouds,
and the rolling thunder.

2.

The words wild lovers say
draw the honeybees near.

The hive they build
is made from their longing,

woven of passion and grief. Someone
steps forward, and the whole dance

begins. The planets draw near,
and all the revolving stars.

This can go on for days.
Dancing skirts

made of muslin or jute, it doesn't
matter. Nakedness is good for love too.

And honey
fresh from the woods,

made from the dew
of longing and love.

3.

When the time is right,
dandelions two inches across

unfold, and the bees come, dozens,
in long lines. Each bee

is fat as a thumb,
attentive as Krishna around Radha.

What they make
is a child,

a nest, a garden. The child
becomes part of the wild,

what is untamed, unnameable.
She sits down in the garden.

The music she makes
resembles the sound of wings

rising
in the other world.

I look down at the earth nest of the mud dauber wasp. It is built in a sort of pyramid, with small birth caves stacked on top of one another, like tiny swaddling cocoons. The doors of the caves have been eaten away, and inside each cave I can just make out what was left behind, an amber shell still holding the print of tiny wings.

*

At the back, near the floor of the nest is a larger cave, where a mother of the next generation might have slept. She was a mother like her own, who would never know her sons and daughters, but would care for them in pre-birth, building their caves in the shape of organ pipes, stocking their caves with spiders and flies. And after she left for good the young woke from their larval sleep, and fed, and spun, and grew—millimetre by millimetre— changed from inside by the intelligence of their own cells.

*

Since this nest was abandoned in the rafters, four generations have come and gone. Even the wasp's great-granddaughter has long since died. Her body now is dust gathered on the floor of the collapsing shed. Somewhere the remains of one wing rise like a sympathetic chord, remembering the paths of the air.

THE THIN PLACES (REPRISE)

In the thin places
my grandmother rocks
her eighty-year-old daughter
back and forth, the cradle of her arms
as wide as the spaces between stars.

THE NIGHT HERON

—for Laurie

The night is moist and lovely,
the crickets talking in the tall grass.

The night heron, waiting in the reeds,
what does he make of all this?

He stands, still
as a stick, and listens.

So it is with me.
I hear the words

you say, and the words
you don't say.

Sometimes grief comes in,
maybe the ecstatic,

a little hint of the music
the universe makes.

I need to ask you this question:
when you say "love,"

why do you weep? Now
you mean everything to me.

Each day
there's always
this amazement:
light coming
over the world again,
somehow making
everything new.
It seems
the dark has passed,
weights and fears
lifted
as if on great wings.
Gabriel is waiting.
Can you see him?
One fire-forged
wing hangs down,
covering
half the world.
He's the one
holding us up,
steadying us
on earth.
We step out.
Light in the Garden,
filling
every cell of our bodies.

ACKNOWLEDGEMENTS

Some of these poems first appeared in *High Plains Literary Review* and *Ellipse*. The poem "The Heaven of Loss" (originally titled "The Great Escape") was commissioned by CBC Radio for their Poetry Face Off, February 2003. Many of these poems were part of an earlier manuscript which was a finalist for the CBC Literary Awards, 2003. Many were also written during the tenure of a Creation Grant in 2001. The author thanks the province of New Brunswick, Cultural Branch, for its continuing support. The cover image, reproduced in its entirety above, is after an etching by Dan Steeves, entitled "its resonance deepened with many viewings" (22.7 × 60.3 CM). This print was made from an intaglio etching made on a zinc plate.

¶ This book was typeset in a digital revival of Deepdene, designed by the American type designer Frederic Goudy (1865–1947). Goudy drew the roman letters for Deepdene in 1927, supposedly based on a Dutch type by Jan van Krimpen called Lutetia, which had recently been introduced in America. In Goudy's own words, "I soon got away from my exemplar to follow a line of my own." The colour and texture of Deepdene are distinctive, balancing a modest x-height with apertures which are larger than usual for Goudy. Graceful, warm and even in tone—it is perhaps Goudy's most satisfying roman. The italic, designed the following year, slopes at a mere three degrees. Deepdene was issued for machine composition by the Lanston Monotype Corporation in 1928. The digital version used here was released by the Lanston Type Library, the digital descendant of Lanston Monotype, owned by Gerald Giampa. Deepdene was named after Goudy's home in Marlborough, New York.   AS

POEM INDEX

Gaspereau Press acknowledges the support of the
Canada Council for the Arts and the Nova Scotia
Department of Tourism and Culture.

Typeset in a digital rendition of Monotype Deepdene
by Andrew Steeves. Printed offset, Smyth-sewn &
bound at Gaspereau Press.

5   4   3   2   1

NATIONAL LIBRARY OF CANADA CATALOGUING IN PUBLICATION

Cooper, Allan, 1954–
    Gabriel's wing / Allan Cooper.

    Poems.
    ISBN 1-894031-83-0

    I. Title.

PS8555.O587G33 2004   C811'.54   C2004-900280-5

GASPEREAU PRESS · PRINTERS & PUBLISHERS
ONE CHURCH AVENUE, KENTVILLE, NOVA SCOTIA
CANADA B4N 2M7